Tchaikovsky: The Ballet Suites

BLACK DOG MUSIC LIBRARY

Tchaikovsky: The Ballet Suites

Swan Lake, *Opus 20*

Sleeping Beauty, *Opus 66*

Nutcracker Suite, *Opus 71*

TEXT BY DAVID FOIL

WITH PHOTOGRAPHS OF THE NEW YORK CITY BALLET BY COSTAS

BLACK DOG & LEVENTHAL PUBLISHERS
NEW YORK

Copyright ©1995 Black Dog & Leventhal Publishers Inc.

The enclosed compact disc compilation ℗1995 CEMA Special Markets.
Product of CEMA Special Markets, a division of Capitol Records, Inc.,
1750 N. Vine St., Los Angeles, CA 90028

Published by
Black Dog & Leventhal Publishers Inc.
151 West 19th Street
New York, NY 10011

Distributed by
Workman Publishing Company
708 Broadway
New York, NY 10003

Designed by Martin Lubin and Allison Russo

Special thanks to Judith Dupré

Book manufactured in Hong Kong

ISBN: 1-884822-39-8

FOREWORD

*T*he highly romantic ballet music of Tchaikovsky endures for generations as some of the most popular symphonic works in the Western world. In this volume you will be able to read and learn about Pyotr Ilich Tchaikovsky, the man and the composer; you will better understand the importance, the meaning, and the structure of his great ballet works; and you can enjoy and listen to the music as you read.

Play the compact disc included on the inside front cover of this book and follow along with the musical commentary and analysis. Please note that the times of the relevant musical passages are noted for your convenience.

Enjoy this book and enjoy the music.

To call Pyotr Ilich Tchaikovsky (1840–1893) a misunderstood composer might seem absurd. As far as the public is concerned, and has been for more than a century, he is one of the best-loved composers Western music has ever produced. Though popular opinion would probably rank him as a master on a par with Mozart, Bach, Beethoven, and Wagner, academic and critical opinion have been in violent disagreement during the twentieth century about his relevance as a creative artist. Surprisingly for a composer of his reputation, Tchaikovsky has been dismissed by some who have judged his music trite, sentimental, and not worthy of consideration.

His Life

The facts of Tchaikovsky's life are not as well known as the gossip about it, a state of affairs that has probably served to compromise critical opinion of his work. In many ways he was a tormented soul: a homosexual in a society that held stunningly hypocritical views on the subject, a neurotic who had to deal with a number of personal catastrophes and tangled relationships, an esthete with decidedly European interests at a time when Russian nationalism was the prevailing musical style in his society.

In his privileged social circle in Czarist Russia, where homosexuality was otherwise a capital crime, Tchaikovsky's sexual proclivities do not seem to have been a life-and-death matter. Though he made a disastrous marriage to a confused woman and conducted a fascinatingly strange relationship

Pyotr Ilich Tchaikovsky (1840–1893)

Palace near Moscow. Tchaikovsky was part of a privileged social circle in Czarist Russia.

with his patroness, Mme. Nadezhda von Meck, Tchaikovsky enjoyed the company of many friends and a loving family. Though he lived only for fifty-three years—to this day, the circumstances of his death in 1893 remain in question—he enjoyed an abundant and productive life.

As a composer, Tchaikovsky was anything but a prophet without honor in his own country. Some of his contemporaries scoffed at his well-known respect for European culture and the way he deified Mozart above all other composers. To their way of thinking, his music was not sufficiently "Russian." But Tchaikovsky's music

Three of the Mighty Five (clockwise from top): Cui, Mussorgsky, and Rimsky-Korsakov.

is—in its character and soul, as well as in its rhythms, sonorities, and instrumental colors—as "Russian" as that of the five great nationalist composers of his day: Modest Mussorgsky, Aleksandr Borodin, Mily Balakirev, César Cui, and Nikolay Rimsky-Korsakov. Tchaikovsky's relationship with this school of composers, known as the Mighty Five, was a complicated one. Perhaps the thing about him that most antagonized them was his formidable skill as a composer; he wrote and orchestrated with amazing speed, astonishing consistency, and a technical authority that can only be described as virtuosic. In that, he was very close to his beloved Mozart.

The conductor Leonard Bernstein once said that Tchaikovsky was always writing songs, regardless of the form—that there are songs in his symphonies, concertos, chamber music, and ballets, as well as in his operas and the art songs he composed. That would certainly explain the popularity of his music—as well as its most frequent criticism that it is too accessible. The sumptuous melodies and nakedly expressive arc of Tchaikovsky's last symphony do not entrance musicologists and critics as do the rigorous architecture and formal detachment of Brahms's last symphony, for instance. Were he still alive, Tchaikovsky's response might well be "So what?" He was clear about his own tastes, even if they appalled the conservative. He was not being disingenuous when he declared that Leo Delibes's charming ballet *Sylvia* was worth more to him than Wagner's entire operatic cycle, *Der Ring des Nibelungen*. (Tchaikovsky attended the cycle's premiere in 1876 in Bayreuth, where Wagner failed to make to time to greet him.) And though he met and liked Brahms personally—Brahms remained in Hamburg once to hear him conduct, and they shared a pleasant, drunken lunch—Tchaikovsky found his music pompous and empty; he much preferred the charm of Grieg.

As is usual with great artists, the dark side of Tchaikovsky's life animated his genius. The terrible anxiety that plagued him suggests an emotional life of great depth and sensitivity. Who else, in a decorative piece called "Waltz of the Flowers" in a diverting ballet called *The Nutcracker,* would have included a contrasting section in which the lower strings seem to sob in anguish? The result is to give the music's surface beauties a dramatic context—a flip side, so to speak. Because of the awareness of his sexual preferences and his nakedly emotional style, Tchaikovsky has been described since his death as a hysterical or effeminate composer. But the careful control he exercises in his music—which freely acknowledges a feminine element as well as a powerfully masculine one—is virile and exact, hardly hysterical. It is so beautiful that, even today, it has the power to get under one's skin, and perhaps embarrass the listener with the emotional response it evokes.

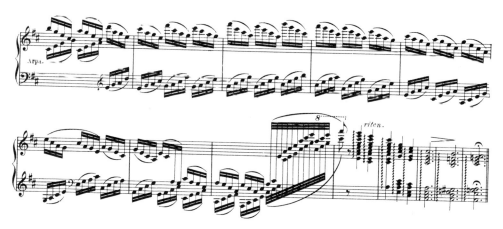

"Waltz of the Flowers"
from **The Nutcracker.**

The Ballet Scores

These varied aspects of Tchaikovsky's personality are powerfully present in his ballet music. The sophistication, inspiration, and symphonic unity of his scores for *Swan Lake, Sleeping Beauty,* and *The Nutcracker* redefined ballet music, raising it to a level it had never before attained. However, ballet actually occupied little of the time he spent composing, and only *Sleeping Beauty* achieved definitive success in his lifetime. *Swan Lake* was such an overwhelming achievement that audiences and dancers did not catch up with it until the choreographer Marius Petipa's famous revival in St. Petersburg in 1895, some twenty years after its premiere and two years after Tchaikovsky's death.

It is wrong to dismiss Tchaikovsky as merely a ballet composer. He brought to ballet music, as a serious composer, the qualities it so badly needed at the time—a sophisticated musical plan of great breadth, consistent melodic inspiration, and skillful exploitation of the expressive means of the orchestra. Ballet composers in Imperial Russia tended to be hacks, writing music much as seamstresses cut material—by the yard, trimmed to fit. Anyone who has had to listen to the music of Cesare Pugni, Ludwig Minkus, and Riccardo Drigo knows how dreary it can be, though it continues to this day to inspire great dancers. The power at the ballet in Imperial Russia resided with the ballet master, and ballet masters were not interested in genius composers. A surviving contract for Alexander Serov, a now forgotten composer who worked with Petipa, lays out the terms in humiliating detail: The music must conform to the ballet master's image of the work, the

The Bolshoi Theater, Moscow

composer must be present ("without fail") and willing to make cuts during rehearsals, and he must do all of this "without protest."

Tchaikovsky was well paid for his ballets, and there is no indication that he had to endure such indignities. But it is known that the *Swan Lake* premiere so challenged the original orchestra members that they substituted some of Pugni's music where Tchaikovsky's left them simply mystified.

SWAN LAKE

Contrary to some accounts, *Swan Lake* was not a disaster in its 1877 premiere at the Bolshoi Theater in Moscow. The ballet had its origins in an entertainment the composer whipped up for his sister's children during a holiday in 1871. Four years later he received a commission for a ballet and used the children's diversion as the basis for a serious work. He used some of the music he had written in 1871 and pulled in melodies from other works he had abandoned, such as his opera based on the Ondine legend. Rehearsals dragged on for weeks, with the dancers, among others, complaining that the music was not *dansante,* or congenial to dancing. The original production certainly seems to have been a mess, saddled with a ballerina past her prime, a choreographer who was not up to Tchaikovsky's level, and an orchestra that simply could not play the score. Tchaikovsky's brother blamed the conductor for its failure, but it appears that the conductor got more of it right than the orchestra. The opening night audience seems to have liked the music—one review suggested that the composer must have come away with a sore waist from bowing and sore ears from all the applause. Still, the results were not completely encouraging—another review described the choreography as an arrangement of "gymnastics exercises." Ever the neurotic, Tchaikovsky was sure the failure was his fault. When he heard Delibes's score for *Sylvia*, he wrote that *Swan Lake* seemed "poor stuff" by comparison.

Pyotr Ilich Tchaikovsky

THE NUTCRACKER

The Nutcracker, amazingly, was an even greater flop. One of Tchaikovsky's last works, it was composed as half of an evening that included the opera *Iolanta.* The double bill was premiered in St. Petersburg in 1892, though some of the ballet music had already received great acclaim from concert audiences who had heard one of the two enduring suites he drew from the score. The evening was roundly panned by critics and audiences. Part of the failure may have been due to the absence of the choreographer Petipa, who had made *Sleeping Beauty* such a triumph two years earlier. Petipa wrote the scenario for *The Nutcracker,* but the choreography was left to Lev Ivanov and the results were apparently uninspired. Tchaikovsky himself dismissed the *Nutcracker* music contemptuously before the premiere. "It is incomparably inferior to *Sleeping Beauty,*" he wrote to his nephew, adding, "I have no doubt about this." *The Nutcracker* does seem like a clever bauble when compared to the epic drama of the composer's other two ballets. Its first act is heavily burdened with long sequences of mime, and the substance of the ballet is nothing but a string of diversions. But the music, despite Tchaikovsky's feelings, is brilliantly effective even out of context. Though the ballet itself did not find a place in the repertoire until British and American ballet companies made it a Christmas tradition in the mid-twentieth century, the *Nutcracker* suites have always been among the composer's most popular works.

SLEEPING BEAUTY

Sleeping Beauty is unquestionably Tchaikovsky's ballet masterpiece, arguably the finest ballet score written until the advent of Igor Stravinsky (who

Darci Kistler as Princess Aurora in **The Sleeping Beauty.**

revered Tchaikovsky and his ballet music). It is a ballet and a score of epic size and luxuriant detail, testing the resources of even the greatest ballet companies. An impresario, Ivan Vsevolozhsky, had the idea for *Sleeping Beauty.* As the administrator of the Imperial Ballet in St. Petersburg, he contracted Tchaikovsky and Petipa to create the ballet; their first collaboration, and a successful one, *Sleeping Beauty* would have enormous influence on the direction ballet took. Tchaikovsky made a careful study of other successful ballet scores, notably that of Adolphe Adam for *Giselle.* By incorporating leitmotifs (recurring musical phrases that describe a person, place, or state

New York City Ballet corps as the Snowflakes in **The Nutcracker.**

of mind) in *Sleeping Beauty*, the collaborators integrated music, story, and dance in a narrative line in a way that had never before been achieved, realizing ballet's potential as an expressive medium. The results stunned and thrilled audiences (even if Tchaikovsky anguished over the fact that Czar Alexander III, one of his great admirers, had greeted him with only a curt nod after the dress rehearsal). The original production was, by all accounts, magical and utterly worthy of the music itself.

Never again would Czarist society see a night like that. Soon Tchaikovsky would go abroad, finding wealth and acclaim in Europe, and the Soviet revolution would put an end to the glamour of Imperial court society, a world Tchaikovsky clearly loved and made the stuff of legend in *Sleeping Beauty*.

BALLET AS A DANCE MEDIUM

Since Tchaikovsky wrote his ballet music expressly for certain dance forms, the music sometimes takes on the name of the dance itself. Some clarification is in order.

Ballet terminology remains in French (as musical terminology remains in Italian), and that was the fashion in Tchaikovsky's day. The word *pas* means step, as in a dance step, so a *pas de deux* is a dance for two; *pas de trois,* a dance for three; *pas de quatre,* a dance for four; and so on. The *pas de deux* usually observes the following structure: an entrée and adagio (a substantial passage for both dancers called the presentation), followed by a variation for the ballerina, a variation for the *danseur* (male dancer), and a lively coda in which they once again dance together. A *divertissement* is a diversion or entertainment, a brief interlude apropos of nothing in the plot. The second act of *The Nutcracker* is made up of a series of *divertissements,* and they are also employed to great effect in Aurora's wedding celebration in the final act of *Sleeping Beauty*.

Because ballet is a dance medium and not a musical one, and because the great Romantic ballets are all in the public domain, choreographers and impresarios tend to be flexible about what they use of a ballet's score or scenario and how they use it.

Where the musical element completely controls what happens in an opera house, it serves a subsidiary role in a ballet company. For that reason some scores, even Tchaikovsky's (though to a lesser extent), are altered for performance. Individual numbers may be abridged, eliminated, moved, or transferred to different characters. *Sleeping Beauty* poses special problems for most ballet companies because of its scenic demands, the depth of skill it requires of a corps de ballet, and the number of soloists for which it calls. Some companies simply perform its celebratory third act, with its endless *divertissements* and great *pas de deux,* as *Aurora's Wedding. The Nutcracker* is also freely adapted and altered. Depending on the production, the changes either reflect a choreographer's vision (such as Mark Morris's postmodern version, *The Hard Nut)* or are made to accommodate the level of skill of the company. For these reasons, descriptions of the individual numbers in this collection may vary from those you have experienced.

The Recordings

SWAN LAKE, *Op. 20*

The story of Swan Lake is taken from elements of a German fairy tale titled "The Stolen Veil" which appears in J.K.A. Musäus's collection *Volksmärchen der Deutschen.* It is about the love of Prince Siegfried for the beautiful Princess Odette, who has been bewitched by her evil stepmother and the knight Rotbart. The spell has transformed Odette into a swan that regains human form for only a few hours each night at the stroke of midnight. The only means of breaking the spell is a vow of marriage taken in the face of death. Siegfried and Odette meet when he and his friends are out hunting late one evening and become entranced by the swans that glide across a moonlit lake. When the hunters take aim, the swans are transformed into beautiful young women, led by the Princess Odette. Rotbart is lurking in the shadows, keeping a beady eye on Siegfried, who is at once captivated by Odette. She returns his love, and he begs her to attend the ball the following day at which he must choose a bride. Odette and her friends retire to a temple by the lake and, moments later, become swans once again.

At the ball Siegfried endures the festivities and the presentation of six princesses, one of whom he is expected to choose; he refuses them all. His heart leaps when Odette arrives on the arm of Rotbart—only it isn't Odette, it is Rotbart's daughter, Odile, disguised as the hapless princess. Bewitched, Siegfried asks Odile to marry him. Suddenly the hall in the palace grows dark as Rotbart transforms himself into an owl and flies away, screeching in

(L to R): Stephanie Saland, Nina Fedorova, Bonnie Borne, and the New York City Ballet corps in Swan Lake, Act II.

triumph. Through a window Siegfried glimpses a swan gliding across the lake in the moonlight. It is Odette. Realizing his mistake, the young prince flees in horror.

A heartbroken Odette is consoled by her friends. Siegfried, now desperate, rushes through a violent storm that is Rotbart's doing, in search of his beloved.

He finds her and begs her forgiveness, which she grants him. But it is too late: Grief has devastated Odette, and she dies in Siegfried's arms. In a final gesture of evil, Rotbart causes the waters to rise and engulf the tragic lovers. When the storm passes, the surface of the lake becomes smooth and the swans once again appear, an image of tranquil beauty at the heart of a tragic love story.

ACT I—NO. 5 *Pas de deux.* A brilliant fanfare introduces the *pas de deux* (danced generally by a pair of revelers at the celebration of Prince Siegfried's birthday in Act I), hinting at the genial waltz melody of the strings (6 0:11) which bubbles with a lively contrast (6 0:41). The waltz melody returns (6 1:10) in the lower strings and winds, with the violins and flute playing a lightly exuberant counterpoint, all of which effervesces in a rapid upward rush of the strings (6 1:38). The andante section begins (7 0:01) with a suave violin solo with gypsy accents that is presented in a straightforward manner, then decorated in virtuosic fashion in its repeat (7 0:43). The soloist reaches deep into the low register (7 1:28) for a sensuous passage, then rises again to embellish the theme. This episode ends in a trill leading to an orchestral restatement of the solo's original melody (7 2:12), which the soloist then embroiders. Over tremolo strings, the violinist sweetly meditates (7 2:26) on the theme, echoed by the oboe, then breaks into a double-stopped passage (playing on two strings at the same time) that clears the air (7 2:45). The soloist takes up the sweet song once again (7 3:04), leading to another trill, which gives way after a slight hesitation (7 3:35) to the sprightly allegro (7 3:46). The playful tune, again announced by the solo violin, is taken up by the whole orchestra (7 4:08). A minor-key section (7 4:18) features the soloist competing with the trumpet before repeating the playful tune. The music races (7 5:01) to a brilliant conclusion that ends with a bang. A languid waltz tempo returns (beginning of Band 8), with the strings and trumpet answered repeatedly by the clarinets, followed by a chattering of the winds and then the strings ([8] 0:34). The waltz returns ([8] 0:56) with the melody in the lower strings, layered with a rich violin counterpoint and followed by bubbling clarinets. This dialogue is interrupted ([8] 1:23) by sudden chords that lead to the coda (Band 9), with its frenetic tune in the trumpets, which lets up ([9] 0:24) only for a gasping interlude in the winds with the strings playing pizzicato. The polka-like tune returns ([9] 0:41), giving way to a virile, Russian-sounding episode ([9] 0:52), followed by a repeat of the chattering woodwinds ([9] 1:04) and the original trumpet melody ([9] 1:16), before hurtling to a breathless, bravura conclusion.

ACT II—NO. 10 *Scene.* One of Tchaikovsky's most beautiful and typical melodic innovations is the yearning, melancholic song sung here by the oboe over the awed tremble of the strings and rippling arpeggios of the harp. It opens the ballet's second act, suggesting the scenic tableau in which Siegfried and his friends watch the swans glide across the moonlit lake. But something lurks behind this exquisite vision: The mood darkens when the French horns take up the oboe melody ([1] 0:56) and coarsen it, as if to suggest the presence of Rotbart and the cruel fate to which the swans have been condemned. This air of menace is slightly relieved by the warm flood of the strings, which engulfs the melody's rising second strain. A sense of desperation, even panic, begins to creep in ([1] 1:41) and rises to a frenzy ([1] 2:10). The strings shudder and fall away, and the trombone drags the mood down to one of tragic despair. The opening line of the oboe melody is hurled out by the violins ([1] 2:16), echoed forlornly first by the flute and oboe, then by the lower strings and woodwinds ([1] 2:29) over the renewed tremble of the violins, as—with a sense of foreboding—the music fades away.

ACT II—NO. 13 *Dances of the Swans.* A beautiful waltz melody describes the grace of the swans, with comments piped in succession (beginning ②0:26) by the flute, oboe, clarinet, and bassoon, followed by an expressive and lively section (②0:34). The waltz returns richly embellished (②1:22), then modulates (②1:52) into a calmer, more serene mood. The second dance (Band 3) is a charming, piquant melody heard first in the violins, then embellished variously with woodwind solos (such as the comical, stuttering clarinet at ③0:38). Instead of continuing in its languid way, the music suddenly (③1:09) begins to race ahead in a delicate frenzy in the violins, until the whole orchestra picks up the melody (③1:20) and sweeps to a breathless finale.

Darci Kistler and Igor Zelensky as Odette and Siegfried in Swan Lake.

The mood changes again (Band 4), with the bassoons playing a rocking accompaniment upon which two oboes, then two flutes, sing a duet. The strings take up the thread (④ 0:19) and develop it into a smoother melody. The original piping of the woodwinds returns (④ 0:52) and has the last word, punctuated by the whole orchestra. There follows a lengthy section, the *pas d'action,* in which Odette and Siegfried declare their love. A luminously erotic mood is set by glowing chords in the woodwinds (the beginning of Band 5), contrasted by the harp's arpeggios (a device Tchaikovsky used brilliantly), which lead eventually to an accompanying figure that cradles a tenderly ardent violin solo (⑤ 1:01). The rich melody (culled from the love duet in the score of Tchaikovsky's unproduced opera, *Undine)* continues to unfold with gentle comments from the orchestra and ends gracefully. The woodwinds and lower strings (playing pizzicato) give out a breathless subject (⑤ 2:31) that serves to connect the more expressive string solos. The solo violin returns with a livelier waltz melody (⑤ 3:00) that wavers emotionally between joy and sorrow; it is repeated and embellished, and the breathless woodwind subject returns for contrast. The solo cello (⑤ 4:50) takes up the violin's solo, joining the violin in a duet that usually reflects the adagio partnering onstage of Odette and Siegfried. The tempo changes suddenly (⑤ 6:37) with a lively musical figure that is repeated variously in the strings and woodwinds, rising higher and growing bolder as its speed increases, bringing the scene to a sparkling conclusion.

ACT III—NO. 20 *Hungarian Dance (Czárdás).* This is one of the brief, colorful national dances (along with those of Spain, Italy, Russia, and Poland) heard in Act III at the ball where Siegfried is tricked into the betrothal to Odile. Based on the *hajdútanz* (a folk dance of the Heiducks), the *czárdás* is a dance form that became popular in Hungary in the 1830s. Loosely structured, the *czárdás* follows a slow-fast pattern: *the lassu,* the deliberate and melancholy introduction (beginning here after the introduction at [10] 0:17), alternates with a corresponding fast section called the *friss* or *friszka* ([10] 2:07), which usually involves wild steps and spins. Tchaikovsky captures the contrasting moods with typical dash and orchestral color.

SLEEPING BEAUTY, *Op. 66*

Tchaikovsky and Petipa turned to the French fairy tale "La belle au bois dormant" by Charles Perrault for the inspiration of *Sleeping Beauty,* a work that celebrates the nobility of royalty in a way that made its premiere a signal event in Czarist St. Petersburg. The curtain rises on the splendid christening of the Princess Aurora in the court of King Florestan XXIV. Catalabutte, the master of ceremonies, welcomes the guests, including the Lilac Fairy, her retinue of fairies, and their cavaliers. The fairies present gifts to the infant with the promise that she will have a happy and fortunate life. The atmosphere changes dramatically with the arrival of a grotesque old fairy, Carabosse, who is livid because she has not been invited. The king tries to calm her, but her hatred is all-consuming. She is determined to deliver her gift—the curse of death—to the infant princess. The Lilac Fairy steps forward, countering Carabosse's curse with the assurance that Aurora will not die but will sleep for a hundred years, a fate that will be triggered by the princess's pricking her finger on a spindle. Only the kiss of a handsome prince will awaken her from her enchanted sleep. Carabosse flees in fury, and the court encircles the child's cradle to protect her.

Years later, Aurora's sixteenth birthday is being celebrated in the kingdom, where, by royal decree, all sharp implements have been banned. Catalabutte is enraged to find a group of old peasant women threading spindles and spinning. The king and queen enter. The king is prepared to condemn the old women to death, but the queen intervenes on their behalf. As Aurora arrives and the official celebration begins, the princess's four suitors step forward, each presenting her with a rose. The mood changes ominously as an old woman appears to present Aurora with a gift. It is discovered too late that the gift is a spindle and the old woman the hated Carabosse—Aurora

Princess Aurora meets the evil Carabosse in **The Sleeping Beauty,** *with Darci Kistler as Aurora.*

Princess Aurora succumbs to her fate in The Sleeping Beauty. *Darci Kistler as Aurora, with Diana White as the Queen and Erlends Zieminch as the King.*

pricks her finger and succumbs to her fate. In the pandemonium that follows, the Lilac Fairy appears, casting a spell of sleep over the entire court and causing a forest of trees and brambles to enclose the palace, hiding it from the outside world.

A century passes. A playful entourage accompanies the distracted Prince Florimund on a hunt. The prince, beguiled by the atmosphere of the forest, sends his friends on ahead of him. He is stunned by what then materializes before him—the Lilac Fairy, in a mother-of-pearl boat drawn by doves, who tells the prince about the sleeping princess and conjures for him a rapturous vision of her beauty. The prince begs the Lilac Fairy to take him to Aurora, and they depart. The Lilac Fairy leads him through the wilderness to the sleeping beauty. Florimund kisses Aurora, ending the curse. As the prince and princess proclaim their love for each other, the forest vanishes and the court awakens.

The wedding celebration is unequaled in its splendor. The happy couple are entertained by the jewel fairies (Gold, Silver, Sapphire, and Diamond) and a variety of fairy-tale characters (Puss-n-Boots and the White Cat, Cinderella and Prince Charming, the Bluebird and the Flower Princess, and Little Red Riding Hood and the Wolf). The celebration ends with an ecstatic dance by Aurora and Florimund, who live happily ever after.

ACT I—NO. 6 *Waltz.* Tchaikovsky loved the waltz and made particularly eloquent use of it, nowhere more so than in this exquisite melody that appears in Act I as the guests are gathering for Aurora's birthday. A brilliant introduction builds anticipation, then recedes as the waltz begins (11 0:33). The waltz, a gently swaying melody given out by the strings, is followed by a lively second strain (11 1:06), punctuated by lightly sounded brass chords. The melody returns with ecstatic accents from the woodwinds before a new melody (11 2:10) appears in the flute and glockenspiel. The original theme returns (11 2:40), and the entire waltz is repeated before spinning to a splendid conclusion.

ACT I—NO. 8 *Pas d'action (The "Rose" Adagio).* One of the ballet's most breathtaking moments is this grand adagio in which Aurora is presented with roses by four suitors at her sixteenth birthday party. A pulsing figure in

The joyful wedding of Princess Aurora and Prince Florimund in The Sleeping Beauty *with Darci Kistler and Damian Woetzel.*

the horns, joined by the oboes, introduces another of Tchaikovsky's voluptuous harp cadenzas (12 0:11) and ends with a grand pause. The harp is joined by the woodwinds to create a rich arpeggio accompaniment (12 0:46), upon which an achingly lovely melody is set (12 0:52) by the massed violins. The second strain of the melody (12 1:24) takes a different turn into a more melancholy mood which is defused by a passage that seems filled with uncertainty (12 1:45). Over the trilling in the strings and woodwinds, hints of the original melody return (12 2:25), and the intensity rises. With energetic, upwardly rushing phrases in the orchestra (12 2:52), the original melody is swept back into place (12 3:09) with greater emphasis. It runs its course, giving way to another, echoing phrase in the lower strings (12 3:29). The woodwinds then take over (12 3:46) with a delicate interlude until the bass enters (12 4:07) to signal the return (12 4:27) of the original melody, transformed here by cymbal crashes and a relentless climb to a sumptuous coda (12 5:05).

ACT III—No. 25 *Pas de quatre (The "Bluebird" pas de deux).* Among the many diversions at the wedding of Princess Aurora and Prince Florimund is a brilliant *pas de quatre*, usually dominated by a fabulous solo for the Bluebird, performed by a male dancer. A colorful, darting melody for the flute (joined by the clarinet) sets the tone here, before the violins and woodwinds (13 0:40) add a somber edge to the vibrant mood.
The cheerful tune returns (13 1:25), this time led by the clarinet. With comments from the woodwind solos, the orchestra brings the opening section (13 1:53) to a close. The variation of Cinderella and Prince Charming begins (13 2:18) with an insistent figure in the strings that develops into a vigorous waltz (13 2:22), with strong accents from the brass. A repeated,

rising phrase (beginning at 13 2:45), a favorite Tchaikovsky device, ends the brief waltz. The variation of the Bluebird and the Flower Princess (so fiendishly difficult that it gives the entire *pas de quatre* its name) begins (13 3:03) with a swooping melodic figure in the flute, accompanied by the clarinet in a charming manner, before the whole orchestra joins in (13 3:32) with fluttering woodwinds and pizzicato strings to create the image of birds in flight. Over a pizzicato string accompaniment (13 3:46), a second flurry of sonic images is established by a dizzying theme in the strings, with comments from the clarinet and the other woodwinds, that grows in intensity and brilliance.

THE NUTCRACKER, *Op. 71*

Marius Petipa devised the scenario for *The Nutcracker,* though illness prevented him from designing the choreography. His source was *"Der Nussknacker und der Mäusekönig"* ("The Nutcracker and the Mouse-King"), a story by the German writer, critic, and *bon vivant* E.T.A. Hoffmann (of *Tales of Hoffmann* fame). Though the scenario of *The Nutcracker* has been adapted and altered in various ways, the profile of this slight but appealing story remains fairly constant. A Christmas celebration is under way in the well-stuffed Biedermeier home of a happy, bourgeois family. In the midst of the usual holiday chaos of family and guests, daughter Clara (in Russian productions she is called Mary, Marie, or Masha) greets her godfather, a curious old man named Drosselmayer. He presents her with a handsome nutcracker. Later that night, as Clara sleeps with the nutcracker, she dreams she that saves the day in a battle against the King of the Mice and his unsavory minions. In gratitude, the nutcracker transforms itself into a handsome

Drosselmayer and the Nutcracker in The Nutcracker.

prince, who whisks her away on an exciting adventure. Passing through a snowstorm, they arrive at the Kingdom of Sweets (or Confiturembourg), where the Sugar Plum Fairy regales them with a mind-boggling entertainment that includes Arabs serving coffee, dancing mirlitons, Russians spinning in a trepak, and waltzing flowers. The party ends triumphantly with the Sugar Plum Fairy and her Cavalier dancing in Clara's honor, bringing an enchanting dream to a blissful conclusion.

OVERTURE The magical mood of the ballet effervesces in this quicksilver mini-overture, scored for a delicate dazzle of strings (violins and violas only) and woodwinds, that reflects Tchaikovsky's affection for classical music, especially Mozart's. The strings dominate, both in the spirited first theme and in its capering embellishments. After a sudden, questioning turn of phrase in the woodwinds (14 0:39), the sensuous, deliciously arching countermelody (14 0:47) gives way to happy hysteria, after which (14 1:34) everything is repeated.

ACT I—NO. 2 *March.* The children at the Christmas party are hard at play, having organized themselves into troops that march around the Christmas tree. Toylike, muted fanfares, heard in the orchestra with *pizzicato* (plucked) lower strings scampering along wittily beneath the melody, alert us to the oncoming parade. After another wave marches by, the woodwinds take over (15 1:09) in an urgent interlude that suggests impending "battle." Sure enough, it breaks out (15 1:22), with the fanfares bolstered by gusts of sound sweeping upward in the strings and finishing in the flutes.

ACT II—NO. 12 *Coffee (Arab Dance).* In the ballet's second act, we are in the Kingdom of Sweets, where Clara is diverted by exotic Arabs bearing coffee. The muted strings pulse quietly with a smoldering effect, while the woodwinds sigh and purr. A sultry melody rises in the strings ([16] 0:26), and shivery taps from the tambourine add to the music's mystique. The oboe and the English horn sing out in alluring arabesques ([16] 2:14). The pulsing continues as the melody and its decorations fade, and the music exits as mysteriously as it entered.

ACT II—NO. 12 *Trepak (Russian Dances)/Dance of the Mirlitons.* An unmistakably Russian dance hurtles into view (Band 17), inspired by the trepak, a high-spirited Ukrainian dance for men that is famous for its squats and wild split leaps. The euphoria grows quickly into a frenzy, and the dance concludes with a breathless "Ha!" Next comes the *Dance of the Mirlitons* (Band 18), an airy duet for two flutes that pauses slightly as the flutes flutter over the sob of the English horn. The duet quickly resumes, reaching a sprightly end, when the music suddenly gives way ([18] 1:11) to a strange interlude with an oddly swinging rhythm and a rising, minor-key melody in the trumpet and then in the strings. The flutes return ([18] 1:39), blithely echoing their earlier duet and reasserting—effectively this time—the sprightly ending.

ACT II—NO. 13 *Waltz of the Flowers.* The woodwinds repeat a melody that reaches up, up, up, with an emotional effect, until the harp clears the air ([19] 0:17) with its cadenza of sparkling arpeggios. The horns announce the noble, somewhat questioning waltz theme ([19] 0:52) hinted at earlier by the woodwinds. The clarinet comments on it, linking it to the genial, gracious melody with which the strings answer ([19] 1:24), the flute and oboe trilling

Diana White as Coffee in **The Nutcracker.**

in agreement. The elements are repeated, embellished, and handed off variously, with ever-increasing ease and assurance, until another inquiring melody sung by the flute and oboe introduces a contrast ([19] 2:51). Suddenly a fit of melancholy rocks the euphoric mood ([19] 3:19)—the violas and cellos weep and sob, in a manner much like that of the exquisitely expressed anguish that opens the Letter Scene of Tchaikovsky's opera *Eugene Onegin*. The anxiety begins to fade ([19] 3:47), and the principal waltz theme returns ([19] 4:08), this time concluding the dance with brilliant, rapturous energy.

ACT II—NO. 14 *Pas de deux.* The presentation of the *pas de deux* begins over the harp's arpeggios with a disarming melody heard in the cellos ([20] 0:13), a simple, descending scale that is developed into a kind of song before the woodwinds and other strings take it up, the cellos echoing a phrase in counterpoint. The music suddenly becomes airborne ([20] 1:46), with an ardent variation from the oboe and then the bass clarinet, as the horns sigh in support and the strings and the harp sweep delicately about. The strings pick up the melody, bringing it to a passionate level of expression ([20] 2:32), from which the trumpets and trombones march down to a point where a series of warm chords ([20] 2:48) accompany the splendidly decorated return of the descending-scale subject, now heard throughout the orchestra. The music begins to relax with a sensuous stretch in the strings ([20] 3:36), before the woodwinds take flight ([20] 4:10) to close the first section. A brief variation (for the Sugar Plum Fairy's Cavalier) is heard in the woodwinds and strings (Band 21, through [21] 0:41). The famous variation

Valentina Kozlova and Igor Zelens as the Sugar Plum Fairy and her Cavalier in **The Nutcracker.**

for the Sugar Plum Fairy begins ([21] 0:43), featuring the magical sound of the celesta heard over the muttering of the woodwinds and strings. The buoyant coda begins (Track 23) with an energetic theme in the violins, decorated by the flutter of woodwinds, over the racing pulse of the horns. A contrasting section ([22] 0:24) adds to the giddy mood, with the violins brilliantly garlanding a smart, melodic figure in the bass. All this is repeated ([22] 0:41), more riotously and with great vigor, bringing the pas de deux to a close.

ACT II—NO. 8 *Waltz finale.* Clara's euphoric dream of her visit to the Kingdom of Sweets is summed up in this sweeping, joyous waltz, so typical of Tchaikovsky's style at its most gracious. A series of charismatic episodes (beginning at [23] 1:23) summons all the pleasures she has seen and sampled before the waltz resumes ([23] 2:32) and rises to a glorious finale ([23] 2:59). Over a sudden tremolo in the strings ([23] 3:24), the music that accompanied Clara's arrival begins to bear her and the Nutcracker Prince away—out of her dreams and back to reality—as the Sugar Plum Fairy, her Cavalier, and the citizens of the Kingdom of Sweets wave farewell.